The Journey That Never End

The Journey That Never End

A Luther Fraser Story

ReadersMagnet, LLC

The Journey That Never End
Copyright © 2020 by Luther Fraser

Published in the United States of America
ISBN Paperback: 978-1-951775-08-7
ISBN Hardback: 978-1-951775-09-4
ISBN eBook: 978-1-951775-10-0

All rights reserved. No part of this publication may be reproduced, stored in a retrieval system or transmitted in any way by any means, electronic, mechanical, photocopy, recording or otherwise without the prior permission of the author except as provided by USA copyright law.

The opinions expressed by the author are not necessarily those of ReadersMagnet, LLC.

ReadersMagnet, LLC
10620 Treena Street, Suite 230 | San Diego, California, 92131 USA
1.619.354.2643 | www.readersmagnet.com

Book design copyright © 2020 by ReadersMagnet, LLC. All rights reserved.
Cover design by Ericka Walker
Interior design by Shemaryl Evans

Book One

Characters

Maternal Grandmother: Iva Vanterpool

Mother: Anta Amos

Aunt(s): Gladys Thourbourne
 : Corina Chinnery
 : Patricia Chinnery
 : Irene Chinnery

*Uncles

Paternal Granparents: Zacarihrra Fraser
 Elizabeth Fraser

Father: Luther D. Fraser Sr.

Uncle(s): Gustave Fraser
 : Charles Fraser

Aunt: Keturiah Fraser

Prelude

The Journey That Never Ends is a novel written about a child whose life started from the moment he was conceived. The trials that he faced even in the womb and the many trials and tribulations that he faced growing up from a young man. The journey never seems to end, but it also offers insight to the struggles that one faces every day of our lives.

Be aware that this young child whose parents had abandoned was also abandoned by his maternal grandmother and was tossed from one island to another, only to find himself caught between the devil and the deepest of blue seas.

The Setting

The body of water that separates these two islands is tremendous. All it takes is a boat ride that would take one from the emerald isles of Saint Thomas, one of the United States Virgin Islands, across the way to Tortola, the British Virgin Islands.

My mother whose mother was from the Dominican Republic migrated to the island of Saint Thomas via Tortola. The British West Indies with her four children that includes my mother.

My paternal grandparents was born on Tortola which includes my father, two older brothers, and one sister.

It is unclear when my mother and father met and if it was lust or love that brought them together, but it was also known that my father was a player.

Dedication

A novel that should have been dedicated to the two women in my life, but instead, I dedicate it to their memory, my life, a very unusual life started out with great anticipation, but for no uncertain reason. That life got turned around. At six months pregnant, my mother was abandoned by her lover (my father). She in returned abandoned the child that she was carrying (me) and could not wait to finally be rid of the burden that may have caused her to lose her Prince Charming, who deserted her for a better life for himself among the bright lights somewhere in North America.

Chapter 1

No one would believe *The Journey That Would Never End* would continue to the point of no return. Approximately sixty something years ago, a child was born to parents who should not have become parents from the onset of time; the child's father was loved by many people and especially to woman who would easily succumb to his every wishes. My father, who had fathered another son by another woman was a charmer; he had the body for which every woman died for. He must have been hung as a male since I inherited all the things that he once possessed, his charm, his sexual prowess, and an almost dead singer for his twin brother.

My father, and I use the term father very loosely, my father came from parents who had no morals. I learned at a very early age the occupation of my paternal grandparents. My grandfather had never worked a day in his life; his wife and my grandmother lived on an estate on the island of Tortola, the British Virgin Islands. People often wondered how she lived on an estate (a private estate) and did not work. It was also rumored the she worked as a conjure woman, who worked her magic in the cemetery located in Road Town, Tortola. Not much was really known about the Fraser clan, but rumors do travel around the islands; her children, three boys and one girl, kept their lives secretly to themselves most or if not in their lives.

My mother, on the other hand, was a young and naïve woman who fell in love with the youngest Fraser brother; it is unclear as to the length of time their relationship developed, but she soon became pregnant by him, and six months later, he left her to go abroad to better his condition and stature in life. The news to my mother must have been devastating to her. At six months pregnant and left to take care of a child (wow), but on the thirty-first day of December 1945, her lover boarded a boat, an oil tanker that would take him from the harbor of Charlotte Amalie to places unknown to the woman he was leaving or for a better description, abandoning a pregnant woman to satisfy his own quest for a better life.

It must have been shortly before midnight on New Year's Eve when people began to move about the city after church services; most were beginning to celebrate the upcoming New Year's while others were busying themselves with returning to their homes to reflect on the year's past involvements. However, my mother sat on the waterfront with tears in her eyes as the oil tanker began its departure. The spirit of my mother departing her body and traveling with the man she loved.

Three months after her lover's ship set sail, my mother gave birth to a son, her lover's mother; the child's paternal grandmother wasted no time in visiting the child in the hospital maternity ward; she did not stop to see the child's mother but was determined to see the child that her son had made. Reports from the nurses in the nursery was that the child's grandmother stripped the child naked and proceeded to examine the child to make sure that the child was her son's. After a completed examination, the child's grandmother determined that the child was her grandson and she immediately named the child after her youngest son. The things that made the grandmother so sure that the child was her son's was the size of his genital, which showed signs that he was bound to be hung like his father. As soon as her examination was over and after signing the birth certificate naming the child after his father, she immediately left the hospital and returned to her estate on the hellish island of Tortola, the British Virgin Island.

So much had happened in such a short period: my mother lost the love of her life, and in retrospect, I often wondered if my mother was in love for the sake of love or was she infatuated with the size of my father's manhood. His mother named me after his son for which she had no idea that she had done it. To make matters even harder to take and understood. The child's mother suddenly disappeared from the child's life, leaving him to be raised by his maternal grandmother.

Chapter 2

My mother's disappearance from my life was not coincidental. I guess that me being the spitting image of the man she believed she had loved and lost was too much for her to handle, and just as he had abandoned her, she did the same by abandoning me. However, she disappearing from my life and leaving me to be raised by her mother opened up doors that would have remained closed if she had chosen to raise me herself. My maternal grandmother was a woman whose love for money was the greatest thing to ever happen to her; the child's maternal grandmother eventually sent the child to live with his paternal grandparents on their estate across the ocean. After the child's mother's disappearance, the child's grandmother was unable to provide for her grandson and taught it better to part was with her daughter's son, thus relieving her of the burden to try and provide for another mouth to feed.

Life on the other side of the ocean with my paternal grandparents was very odd, and from the onset, I seemed out of place. My grandparents' estate sat on the highest mountain that I had ever seen; there were no neighbors nor neighboring children, most of my days would be spent sitting under the coolness of the trees. While the sun beat down on the hot earth, my nights were mostly spent in fits of sleep and would ultimately be interrupted by my grandparents' mother who did her bidding on the cemetery very late at night. As was mentioned earlier in the novel, no one knew nor did they understand how my paternal grandparents managed to live on an estate, since neither one of them had worked a day in their lives, but as the ordeal continues with my grandmother taking me to the cemetery very late at night, everything that other people rumored about her began to slowly emerge from the darkness of her and my grandfather's life.

Although I was a young child, things did not appear to be right with me in the household that I now reside in. My paternal grandmother slept all day and patrolled the cemetery practically all night. The rituals she performed in the cemetery and the strange noises and voices that emanated in her corner of the cemetery along with the five and smoke that came out of the graves almost made one feel as if they were living through a science fiction movie. After the rituals were ended, my paternal grandmother would be drenched with sweat, she would grab my arm, lead me out of the cemetery for that long and laborious walk back to her estate. She never spoke with me about what or how I was feeling. I guess she thought I was this young and dumb, stupid child. This ritual was performed by her even before I was to become in existence. She performed these graveyard antics with her husband (my grandfather), her three sons, the youngest being my father, and I assumed she did the same with her only daughter (my aunt). These individuals all knew their parents dealing with the cemetery and the dead; they knew how she made her money in order to live on the estate, and they will kept the secret from the men and women they became involved with. But lo and behold, grandmother's secret was about to be blown right out of the water; she was about to be exposed.

Chapter 3

Memory does not serve me as to the many times that I had been abruptly waken from my sleep to accompany my grandmother from her estate (Estate Maize) through the city of Road Town Tortola and eventually to the cemetery where the demons and devils have asleep waiting for God to resurrect them. It seems that as she enters the cemetery, she immediately brings the spirit of the dead, and although there was no one to protect me from my grandmother's way, my constant crying began to have an effect on her attitude toward me. My constant crying was becoming a distraction to her when she took me to the cemetery very late at night. My grandfather was physically there in the home, but he too appeared to be powerless to help me from the ways of his wife, which was understandable, since my grandmother had done the same things to her own children which resulted in her sons leaving their homes at a very early age.

So much had happened in my life since my mother gave birth to me, then abandoned me to her mother and whose mother abandoned me because she claimed that she could not financially provide for her grandson's care which resulted in his paternal grandmother involving me in her work with witchcraft. It seemed as if I was the perfect fit or even a pawn for my paternal grandmother because she immediately indoctrinated me to her way of life. I was immediately placed in her mighty schedule with cemetery duties. There was never any conversation between my paternal grandmother and myself as we took our might from her estate high in the mountain to her work station located in the center of the town of Road Town, Tortola; even after we got to the cemetery, there was no talk. What would a grown woman have to say to a child? The only nonverbal communication that would take between us was for her to sit me down on the nearest grave that she could find as she prepared herself to summons the dead. But as she chanted in a language that was not clear nor understandable to the child, things would begin to happen, things that were very hard for a three-years-old child to comprehend. The longer I went on the mission to the cemetery with my grandmother, the more I began to see and feel the effect of the spirit of the dead; they began to follow and track my every way of life day and night. I had no one to express what I was seeing and feeling my P. grandfather had turned a deaf ear to my crying and my P. grandmother spent all day in her bed after every hard night that she worked on her craft in the cemetery. None of the adults in my life had ever taken an active role in my life, beginning with my mother who I felt had no love to give to me since she had given all the love that she might have understood to the man she loved.

Chapter 4

My crying might have saved my young life from the disastrous ordeal that I have been put through by my paternal grandmother. I guess my crying softened her heart or she simply got tired of me being a constant nuisance in her private space, then suddenly she decided that enough was enough; she decided right then and there that was had to return this child to his paternal grandmother, but her decision came a bit too late. The effect of her working in the cemetery with the aid of dead people had seriously affected me. My once smooth and black skin was now changed to an ashen gray color.

My once black head of hair was now white as snow. My eyebrows and eyelashes matched the color of my hair, and my devilish little playthings had now multiplied themselves from a few to many, many more. (I called the spirits that surrounded me night and day my devilish little plaything.)

My journey back to a maternal grandmother who I did not know and had no semblance of memory of proved to be a task, but the challenges of re-unification was not as challenging as my trip again across the waters to my beautiful home, the US Virgin Islands my paternal grandmother and I became the focus of attention as we boarded the ferry boat that would take us from the British Virgin Island to the United States Virgin Islands.

They stared at us as if we were two people from outer space. I don't recall how long that I had stayed on the estate of my paternal grandparents, but it was long enough to alter my physical outlook but hid the emotions that I had gone through while living with them. My appearance to others when they looked at me was ghostly ghost like. As the ferryboat slowly maneuvered the vast body of water between the Islands, my young mind began to wonder at what lies ahead got to my destination at the dock in the US Virgin Islands (Saint Thomas), the laughter at our presence became louder and more rude and boisterous, but my paternal grandmother paid it no attention. As we left the ferry boat and began our walk to my maternal grandmother's home, my paternal grandmother finally spoke to me, almost in a whisper, "Go through the gate, that is where you will meet your maternal grandmother." What a cruel way to be introduced to someone you didn't know. As the last word left her mouth, she quickly disappeared, leaving me no other choice but to follow her direction that she had given me. The thought of me leaving away from this nightmare briefly crossed my mind, but where would I run to? I was a stranger in a land that was so unfamiliar to me. Going through the gate brought screams from the first individual when she saw me, she thought that she had seen a ghost dressed up in his ghostly apparels. She finally stopped screaming when saw a glimpse of recognizing who the stranger standing in the yard beyond the gate was.

She truly recognized the young child standing in the middle of the road, as she began to scream out the pet name of the child's grandmother. "Manca," she screamed. "Manca," she continued to scream, that finally got the attention of my maternal grandmother who came running to find out what the commotion was also about. As she got close to the once screaming woman, she pointed to the child and asked, "Is that not your grandson?" and as she acknowledge to the screaming woman that the child was in fact her grandchild. The woman immediately stopped screaming and said to the child's grandmother. That all hell was going to break out when the child's mother sees the condition that her son was in. In shame, the child's grandmother took him by his hand and escorted him to her humble abode.

News travels around the small islands quicker than the telephone, and before the dust could settle with the child's return from his paternal grandparents from Tortola, the British Virgin Islands, words had been gotten to the child's mother. And the condition that he was in, the child's mother came running, but her running was all in vain, damages to her son was already done; she could blame no one else for the plight of her son: she seemed to vanish from the face of the earth after giving birth to her son. Father gone, mother disappeared from her young son's life, and her mother left to raise a grandson without benefit of financial support for the son.

Chapter 5

The child's mother came demanding to know and find out about her son but was met by her brother, the child's uncle. In her haste to confront her mother about her child's well-being, she never saw nor did she took the time out to see the child sitting alone by himself in the yard of grandmother's house. Her brother then began to chastise his sister, telling her that she left her son and took off, with no way for anyone to be in contact with her, he continued that she left and expected her mother to care for her responsibilities. "There's you, son," he said. As she turned and saw the child she had given birth to, the disgust came over her and showed on her face. Her brother saw the discomfort on her face and immediately told her to be gone from his mother's house. The answers she came looking for she never got, and like the big bad wolf, she left the yard with her son in tow.

I certainly did not understand back then how a mother could ultimately walk away from a child that she had carried for nine months and, at birth of the child, randomly disappear from that child's life. She knew nothing of what the child had been through during her absence from his life; she was even not aware that her son had been living across the waters with his paternal grandparents, she wasn't even aware that the child was having nightmares and was seeing spirits from the other side. Nonetheless, she was about to be rudely awakened by the child's behavior, a behavior that night made her nearest over taking the child from her mother.

The child's ability to see in the natural and the supernatural world was unknown to the child's mother and his maternal grandmother; no one knew when the child's devilish little playthings would come out to play with the sick child, and tonight might very well be the night for them to show their faces.

The child's mother hurriedly left her mother's home and took the child to an unknown and undisclosed location, she made dinner while the child took his bath; after his bath, the child was fed and later put to bed. And lo and behold as the child began to be at peace and as he got into his sleep pattern, his devilish little playthings interrupted his sleep and came out to play. However, their playing was more intense than he had ever seen before; they jumped on his bed, they climbed on the ceiling and ran up and down the four walls in his room. The child felt threatened by some many of his play things, he began to scream, which brought his mother running to his room; upon entering the room, her son began to ask her if she was seeing these things jumping up and down on the bed. "Mother," the child screamed, "can you see them crawling on the wall and ceiling?" Of course she could not see what her son was seeing since she did not have the ability to see in the natural/supernatural realm. Unable to understand what was happening to her son, she thought that he was losing his mind. The child's mother and grandmother had no idea that the child had been exposed to many, many nights in the cemetery. The child's mother was not even aware that her mother had sent the child to live with his paternal grandparent across the ocean. No one had ever questioned the child about his experience in the island of Tortola; the child became frustrated, realizing that his mother could do nothing to help him with his situation demanded that she take him back to his grandmother's home.

The beast hunted the child day and night. The beast were his devilish little playthings that began the initial introduction to the child the very first minute that his paternal grandmother introduced him to her rituals in the cemetery at midnight.

Chapter 6

The child's mother after experiencing the abnormality of her son's behavior drove to ask questions as she never did before. She spoke with every and anyone she could find to talk to about her son's unusual behavior especially at night. After numerous conversations with the world and public at large, the child's mother came up with the simple diagnosis for her son; she believed that her son was suffering from a breakdown, but a breakdown from what she did not know. She also thought that her son was losing his mind, but again, she did not communicate with her son. Finally, after much questioning and not receiving the answers she wanted and needed, she finally confided with one of her friends who lived on the Island of Saint Croix, the US Virgin Islands. She informed her friend of the nightmarish behavior he displayed; she also told her friend how her son would ask her if she sees his devilish little plaything, jumping, running, and stomping all over his room but to no avail of the child's mother.

Chapter 6

No one knew that my problem started shortly after I was sent to live with my paternal grandparents across the ocean, and I assumed that everyone thought that I was too young to give an account of my time spent on the island of Tortola, and no one bothered to ask me what I had gone through. The child's mother was also clueless as to the whereabouts of her son during her long furlough from him, but as she described her son's behavior to her friend in Saint Croix, her friend opened her eyes to the ideas that perhaps her son had been exposed to the world of witchcraft. This idea completely stunned the child's mother and took her completely off guard. As she wondered how this could be possible, she thought was not the kind of person. She pondered. It did not take her very long to figure out that in her absence, her mother might have sent her son to spend time with his paternal grandparents across the ocean, when she disliked with a passion, but nonetheless, when as a parent, you have abandoned and neglected your responsibilities, then you are left with no one to blame for the trial and perhaps the tribulation your child or children may have to go through.

After many sleepless night and worrisome days, the child's mother was encouraged to bring her son to her friend's home on the Island of Saint Croix. There, her son and her would meet with a medical doctor who was also knowledgeable in the world of occult. The child's mother was warned by her friend that the child was not physically sick, but since the child had spent and great deal of time surrounded by things in the spiritual world, certain influences had imposed themselves on him so that the doctor would take care of his spiritual need.

After several days on the island of Saint Croix, the child was met by the medical doctor, and after the doctor was able to remove the veil that was placed over the young child's eyes, reassuring the child's mother that whatever her son saw before he came to him. He would never see again. The child was now cured of his maladies and was now free to live a normal childhood life, but as one problem resolves itself yet another problem raised its ugly head.

With all that this child had gone through from his inception in the womb to his birth and then his abandonment from his mother and maternal grandmother to yet another abandonment coupled with his isolation from children that might have or could have helped him to understand and know how to communicate with not only with adults but also with children of his own age, sex, and may another topic suitable for child growth and development.

Chapter 7

At five year olds, no one had prepared me for what was about to happen in my non-experience with other children, no one, it seemed, cared enough to have enrolled me in a pre-school setting; it seemed as if no one had even heard about pre-school nor kindergarten, but here I was with none of the adventures of exposure with other children; here I was attending the first year of schooling at the first grade level. I really did not understand what it meant to be surrounded by a large group of children to begin to learn and socialize with other people, never mind a room full of children who had learned to mingle and socialized with other children who had the benefits or pre-school, pre-kindergarten, and perhaps day care or even after-school care. My first day at school was a total nightmare. I spent my day crying, and as good a teacher my first grade teacher was, my discomfort in her class and in the presence of the other children told a very telling story of the first five years of my life.

My first grade teacher, Ms. Francis, had no children of her own but knew right away that I was a child that lacked the basic knowledge and skills needed to function at the first grade level. She also knew that I was a child who had been neglected and left alone, and as the days become increasingly difficult with me in her class, she suggested to the child's mother that she spend the whole school day(s) with the child in the classroom to help him to adjust himself in his new classroom setting; this process went on for several weeks before the child stopped crying, as he re-adjusted and acclimated himself to his teacher and classmates.

The learning process in the first grade was a very slow one; the child could not grasp the knowledge needed to function at his grade level since he lacked the preparations needed to function at the grade level he was suddenly pushed into. One must understand that the prerequisite to the first grade is one when the child is placed in a pre-school and kindergarten setting; it is these levels where children begins to learn the basics (ex. socialization, counting, the alphabet, and on and on), these skills assist the child in helping him to adjust to the level of being able to do and understand the level of his/her next grade in his/her school curriculum.

As the school year dragged on and finally coming to an end, the child was forced to repeat the first grade, simply because the child had not fully understand nor did he function at the grade level that he was assigned to. My second school year in the first grade took on a different scenario, I had learned what was necessary, and at the end of the school year, I was promoted to the second grade. The years went by so fast that before I knew it, I was promoted to the seventh grade. I would be attending the Charlotte Annalie High School which went from grade seventh through twelve. Full of excitement, I would be attending a school where I would be able to mix and mingle with students who were on my grade level, age, and even get to rub shoulders with student who were upper classmen, athletes, sophisticated and full of themselves.

Chapter 8

It seemed as if as I began my school career at the seventh grade level at my alma mater, life began to evolve for me, I began to grow and develop beyond my years. I got involved with every sports and team that was available to me. I got involved with the varsity club and played basketball, volleyball, football (flag), the only sport that I refused to be involved with was track and field; I hated running and thus refrained from this type of sport activity during this time of growth and development, I was now conscious of my now developing body. I was a lean machine that was admired greatly by my peers and even the buddies that was older that I was; as my promotion to the eight (8) grade, my focus on school suddenly did a dip in my sport life. I was now looking at the opposite sex, of course, I was sexual I believed from the moment of conception, but in the eighth grade, it became fun blown; as you may recall, I had always played sports, thus body fat was never one of my issues. I guess it was midway through my second year at my new school (C.A.H.S.) that I met this special girl whom I fell in love with, and although I played the hound dog during my weekends away from school, I was like a saint Monday through Friday, catering to my newfound love.

Life during these times had not been an easy one for me; it became even harder for me as I tried to balance my school responsibilities with my athletic responsibilities along with my weekends of fun with whomever was available to satisfy the sexual cravings that I had at so young an age. I had no one to talk with even at this stage of my life: mother, father, grandmother, everyone had been invisible to me even when I was a young child. I had uncles but could not model my behavior after; they could not even begin to model my set pattern to my life. I had been a loner for all or most of my life. I claimed to be in love but really never truly understood what the word meant. Oftentimes, I have confused sex with love and vice versa. At one time, I felt that if I've sexed you, then it had to be love. The love I had laid smack dab in my penis. This idea came about as a result of my lack of perhaps a male role model, it also stems from the idea of being raised by a female instead of both parents in the home which brings me to the ultimate question. Can a female raise a male child and based on my experience of being raised by a grandmother and a parent who have been mostly absent from my life tells me that the component is not there for females to raise the male children. Thus, my struggles to understand my behavior as it relates to sex and love or love and sex was a bit confusing during this stage of growth and development; nevertheless, as I continued with my struggles, life went on as it usually did.

As I matriculated from the eighth grade to the tenth, my life continued to became a bail. I played the sports that I was mostly interested in, the girls began to notice me more and more, my body had suddenly shot through the ceiling, my now-ripped body began to show the bulges and bumps. That I had never experienced continuously improved, I was sporting a great GRA index, my love life was on point, and the young ladies were more than willing to sex me at a moment's notice. Many of my friends often wondered what was it that drew not only the female sex toward me but also the guys who were not too sure of their sexuality. I was not a jock and I was not the most dashing guy on campus, but I possessed that cool and mysterious demeanor that drew people to me like flies are drawn to honey. I had a personality that was cool, calm, and reserved, I could be trusted, and those were traits that could only be seldom found in special people. I was a special something, if one can truly look at my humble and almost nonexistence.

My junior year in high school was a bit different from my earlier years at my school. I was a junior getting ready to be promoted to my final year of high school. This was the year when every student was getting ready to pursue a degree from college in a discipline that they intended to make a profession of. I've had many interests but was not able to discuss them with an emotional and well-adjusted someone. I could swim, play tennis, basketball, but I had no idea what I wanted to do with my life after high school. My girlfriend, on the other hand, knew that she would be enrolled in the college of her choice right after her graduation, and soon after summer vacation ended, she and I made promises that we would leave the island to pursue our individual studies, but I had no idea what college if any I would be attending; my sophomore, junior, and senior years was never managed by a responsible adult. I was the one doing and managing the affairs of school and my personal life. I was a gifted athlete and had so many talents but did not have the abilities nor the direction in which to channel my life journey.

Chapter 9

The summer of 1969 was a very productive summer for me. I was now a graduate of the class of 1967. My girlfriend was promoted to her senior year in high school so I decided to stay another year in the island and became employed with one of the airlines that serviced the islands of Saint Thomas, Saint Croix, and Puerto Rico. I was hired as a counter agent for Prinair Airline; representatives did not know nor did I disable to them that I would only be working with them for a year. I believe that working for a year after high school would have given me time and money saved for my departure from the islands to mainland New York. Where I can begin to put my life in order, upon arriving in New York City on a blustering rainy evening, I began to search the classified for jobs that I may have been qualified for; as I glanced through the *New York Sunday Globe*, Ma Bell, better known as New York Telephone Company, had advertised for junior engineers to work with senior engineers. I reported that Monday morning, filled out my job application, and was given a battery of aptitude tests to test my knowledge, strength, and abilities in the drafting profession. I passed those tests and was immediately offered a position as junior engineer. In this position, I was responsible for reading cables that were broken or needed repairs, re-drafting work orders for the engineers, splicing cables and identified broken feeder in manholes. In less than one day, I had left the Virgin Islands, traveled to New York City, and immediately handed a job. At nineteen years old, I felt as if I had arrived two months later, my aunt whom I was living with since my arrival offered me the apartment that she was living in and then she moved to another so that I could have my privacy.

After working at New York Telephone Company for one year, I decided to attend college at night, I applied to Bronx Community College, city university of New York, where I began my college career. I began my career by taking courses in liberal arts and science, and after one year and after being introduced to my famed behaviorist Sigmund Freud, I decided that I wanted to become a child psychologist. My decision to study psychology and to become a child psychologist was on the way that I was brought up. I was a child brought up with no sense of direction. I had parents who were not responsible: my father abandoned my mother who after given birth to me disappeared to parts unknown. My grandmother was left with the burden of trying to provide for her own children as well as me. Not being able to provide for me, I was again abandon and shipped off to the mercy of paternal grandparents that I did not know, and although I was able to overcome the early hardships that I had endured, I thought that psychology would help to me to help another to overcome whatever minor or major problems he/she may face with their early childhood development.

My struggles to attend college during the first two years of my college career presented many challenges for me, working all day and attending college at nights was a slow process, and after two years of doing this maneuver, I was determined to change this situation. I wanted to attend college in the mornings and I needed to secure employment (fun time) in the early afternoon directly after my college days ended. I never knew it back then, but I know now that God really answers the prayer of his people, but as the new semester was almost underway and class registrations began to take shape, I was offered an evening position with my employer; that three p.m. to eleven p.m. offered me the opportunity to attend my schooling from eight a.m. to about two p.m. so I got involved with things at college that I could not ordinarily get involved with attending school at night (evening after work).

Chapter 10

Graduation from junior college arrived sooner than I realized. I did not attend my graduation ceremony because my mother could not find the time to put her life on hold to assist me with sharing in my accomplishment which reminded me of my early childhood years where she was constantly not there for me. My aunt, her oldest sister, wanted to attend my graduation ceremony, but I refused her the opportunity to attend and represent her sister. The need for my aunt to be there with me was not an appealing idea; my family had not really cared for me. They always felt that I was a bit pushy and wanted to constantly try to better my non-status in life. Attending computer programming trade school and going to college was not supposed to be a thing that I should be doing. My family members did not attend college; 99 percent of them had never graduated from high school. They lacked ambitions and felt that I should follow to their footsteps.

Because of the way that I was brought up, alone but not a loner, a lack of guidance and discipline, I was the one who was forced to be the disciplinarian of my life, although I was disappointed that my mother did not attend my graduation ceremony. I continued to press on with my studies. The following semester, I enrolled at Herberth H. Lehman College located in the Bronx, New York. I declared my major studies (psychology) and aggressively began taking my courses that would help me to reach the educational goals for myself. Courses in psychological testing, abnormal psychology, social psychology, child growth and development, and development psychology were some of the concentrated courses that was required in order for me to begin preparations for a bachelor degree in psychology with great expectation and a comfortable work environment I worked toward the goal that I had set for myself.

After almost two and a half years at Herberth H. Lehman College and twenty credits away from fulfilling my BS degree requirements, I received a telephone call, a call that shook the foundation of my life. The caller on the other end of the telephone had a message to deliver to me, but found it difficult to explain why they were calling my home. Annoyed and quite disgusted with the manner by which I was rudely awakened by this caller who turned out to be my aunt's husband, I told him point-blank that he continued to have a message but could not disclose it, then I was going to hang up my telephone, hearing the disgust with him on the telephone, he suddenly said to me, "I hate to be bearer of bad news, you just lost your mother." Not really hearing nor understanding what my aunt's husband had just to me, I thanked him and hung up the receiver on my telephone.

Chapter 11

Before receiving the telephone call from my aunt's husband on that cold November 9, 1979, day, I had scheduled a weekend getaway to Washington, DC, but had to cancel due to the call that I had received early on that morning. I got the call that shocked out of my mind; the reality of the call did not register in my mind until ten minutes after I had received it. "You just lost your mother" and then thanking the caller as if he had just paid me a compliment. I hung up my telephone; minutes later, it struck me that the caller informed me that my mother was dead. After finally setting into the news, I began to make frantic calls to my other relatives living stateside and was told that I should call my mother's home and if no answer was gotten, then I should call my grandmother's house. All attempts to reach someone at my mother's home failed, calls to my grandmother's home continued to give me a busy signal after a busy signal.

Trying to reach someone who might give me confirmation to the telephone can that I had received earlier to several nerve-racking hours, but eventually, I got through to my grandmother's home. My aunt (Patricia) answered the telephone on the first ring; when she heard my voice, she started to cry and quickly turned the telephone over to her daughter (Carrie), who told me that my mother was really dead; she informed me that my mother was on her way to work when it started to rain; she claimed that my mother turned back to get her umbrella, but as she inserted the key into her from door, she keeled over and just like that, she was dead.

November 9, 1979, is a day that became encrypted into my whole being; it was the day that my whole life changed; here I was planning a weekend getaway from my job and away from college work and activities, but now faced with leaving college twenty degree credits shy of my bachelor's degree, losing a job that I loved, giving up an apartment that was conducive to my travel to school and work only to return to my hometown. To begin preparation to take care of my mother's remains, being the only child, it was my responsibility to put my mother to rest, take care of her financial responsibilities and still keep in the back of my mind what my goals and aspirations were before I received the news of my mother's passing; because I was her only child, I was placed in charge of going to the hospital to sign her death certificate, I was responsible for her passing to be published with the local radio station (WSTA). From the time I got the news, I was forced to drop everything concerning my well-being and focused at the task at hand with my mother. I could not get a flight out of New York City on November 9, 1979, and was forced to travel from NYC to San Juan, Puerto Rico on November 10, 1979.

Upon arriving on Saint Thomas on November 19, 1979, I was busy running around the island, trying to get all the necessary parts together in an effort to put my mother to rest. It is surprising how death in a family brings out the worst in family members, so many family members reassess into themselves, while other members flashes out and become as dictators as to decisions that has to be made on behalf of the deceased person.

The death of my mother brought out the worst with me, her sisters, her brothers, and most of all, her mother. When I arrived on Saint Thomas the day after my mom's death, I got off the airplane running, as if someone was chasing after with a gun in their hand. My family members refused to support me with preparing for her final resting; my grandmother's major concern was my mother's life insurance policy. The family wanted to have a wake for my mother, but none wanted to help with the wake preparation. Everyone was looking at me (her son) to provide financially for everything they wanted to do. To them, I appeared to be Daddy More Bucks' son, and to this day, people continue to look at me as if I was loaded with money when in actuality, I am just one day away from being homeless.

There was arguments, fussing, crying with myself and the other members of my family, thing were said that could not be taken back; nine days later, my mother was laid to rest and all ties between myself and the rest of my family had been severed. The medical examiner who performed the autopsy on my mother claimed that she died from a massive coronary. I did not believe his report since my mother had never complained of being sick one day in her life; my mother did not die from a broken heart, and God knows she had been through more than most women her age had gone through. The death of my mother was suspicious. I believed that she was killed because all too often, she spoke the truth to individuals who could not take the truth.

Chapter 12

The day that I buried my mother was the same day that I was offered employment with one of the local union in the island. I was offered a position as Union Business Agent whose responsibilities included managing, representing, contract negotiation, and servicing government employees and employees in the private sector. This job was ideal for me since I have had experience as a shop steward for such unions as local 1199 and local 144 based out of New York City. During the first year of my employment, my estranged wife and I got into a shouting match over the child support for my daughter after agreeing on a support settlement that day. The estranged wife called my manager the very next day, demanding that he fire me from my position because I was not paying support for my daughter. When I got to the office shortly after my ex-wife called, my manager called me into his office to discuss the call he had received; after a short discussion with him, it was decided that he could not fire me since my paying or not paying child support had nothing to do with job performance. Disgusted, I requested some time off from the job, time was granted, and I headed straight to the company's attorney's office where divorce papers were quickly filed and serve on this conniving and conceived woman.

Somewhere between the filing of my divorce and receiving the divorce decree and the day of Thanksgiving Day, the following year, I was met with a dreadful car accident en route from my grandmother's home to my rented apartment. It was Thanksgiving morning; I needed to do my laundry, so I parked my things into my car and headed to my grandmother's home. After washing my clothing and hanging them out to dry, I got busy helping my grandmother with the preparation for the family thanksgiving dinner. After dinner was completed and my clothes dried, I decided that I wanted to be alone. I was not into the Thanksgiving spirits that year since it was a year since my mother had suddenly passed away.

My grandmother became upset when I informed her that I won't be spending Thanksgiving with the family but decided that I wanted to by myself; she fought with me over my wanting to leave, but I left anyway. As I traveled from my grandmother's home from the city toward my apartment on that lone and quiet country road, a car coming in the opposite direction, side-swiped my car hitting me from the right front end of my car hitting me from the right front end of my car to the rear end of my car. As I managed to get out of my car and try to see the car that had almost hit me head on, the car had mysteriously disappeared from thin air. (At one minute, the car was there, and another minute, the car was gone.) As I stood there on the side of the road pondering my next move, a car pulled up on the other side of the road; in the car was a friend from my high school days, when he saw the condition that my car was, he exclaimed, "I saw the way that car was going." He thought whoever was driving that car was on a mission to kill someone. My fellow classmate offered me a ride home, but when I got home, I could not stay in my apartment; it seemed as though I was marked for death that Thanksgiving evening. I needed to get out of here. I locked my door and headed on foot back to my grandmother's home.

As I traveled that long and dark country road with the tears running down my face, I reflected on my mother's death and could not help but having odd and strange feeling about what had almost happened to me just an hour earlier. When I finally got back to my grandmother's home, she had already gotten the news of my car accident. My buddy's mother who lives in Antigua, Wisconsin, saw the accident and told him that he needed to call me and bring me to Antigua because there were evil forces working against me. After settling myself, I called my friend and was told that I needed to come right away to Antigua. He also told me that I should check my right hand because something strange had showed itself on my hand upon examination of my right hand. There was a four-corner box resembling that of a coffin that people are buried in for a funeral. I was told to get some Florida water and wash it away. The very next day, I got on the airplane and flew to Antigua where I was met with my friend who took me to see a woman who was versed in the art of voodoo and black magic (witchcraft).

Upon meeting this woman, my nerves were shot, I was downright scared of what was happening in my life, but the woman knew my fear and tried her best to calm me down, but my nerves continued to be on edge, and since calming me became almost an impossible feat, the woman came directly to the point. The woman told me that my mother had not died from a heart attack, she claimed that my ex-wife and her mother had worked their black magic on my mother and had used evil spirits to beat her down. She also informed me that the accident that I was in was really an accident set up with dummy spirits to take my life. My ex-wife and mother wanted me dead the year after my mother had passed. No one understood it better than myself why my ex. And her mother would want my mother dead, truth be told, my mother never knew my then fiancé who later became my wife but hated the idea that I would marry a woman whose name she hated and made no bones about her dislike for her. My mother thought that I should be marrying my high school sweetheart and choose not to come to my wedding. My ex wanted me dead because I loved and enjoyed the company of another woman more than her. Thus her hell-bent determination for wanting to see me dead and tack away in my grave. So much had happened between the year of my mother's death and burial, my employment and my near death the year after, but through it all, I had managed to onslaught of desires to destroy me. And after understanding it all, I knew that there was (are) a higher power that was looking over me.

Chapter 13

My employment with the local union in the Islands was a productive one. I love my job and the work that I was performing for the thousands and thousands of people that the union represented, but my disappointment came after realizing that I was credits (20) away from receiving my college degree shortly before the passing of my mother. My determination to return to the mainland continue to hunt me. To further bring insult to injury, the regional vice president of the Caribbean Islands came to Saint Thomas, slept with a member of the union, and offered at a salary that was higher than I had been receiving. After weeks of trying to get the matter resolved. At the local level, no one wanted to touch the issue. I started a letter writing campaign to the mainland, citing articles and sections of contracts that provides for equal pay for equal work. None of my superiors wanted to help; they said that their hands were tied. Nonetheless, my letter writing campaign that started in the region eventually spoiled over to the mainland and the national treasure.

Soon after my letter writing campaign fell on all deaf ears, I received an invitation to attend a union conference at Piney Point, Maryland. When I got to Piney Point, I approached the regional National Treasurer, the man responsible for the finances of the union; he informed me that I had went about trying to resolve my problem the wrong way. His wrong way meant that I was trying to right a wrong by exposing the matter for what it was. After realizing that he too would not help my cause, I demanded to have an audience with the National President; my request was granted; two days later, I met with the National President, who informed me that he was aware of the problems that I was having with the discrepancy in pay with another writer who was not qualified to do the same job as myself, but was being compensated with a higher salary than I was. He outlined the re-adjustment of my salary and insisted that I would be paid retroactively back to the woman's date of hire and that I would be given a special bonus for the manner by which I continued to function in the job classification that I was hired irrespective of the injustice. That was done to me. I was encouraged by the National President to continue to do the great job that I was doing and reassured me that the changes and benefits will be sitting on my desk when I returned from the conference and back at work in the Caribbean Region (Saint Thomas, U.S.J.I.).

When I returned to work on that following Monday, the changes in my salary along with a bonus check and my adjusted weekly check was sitting there as the National President had instructed. Having my situation rectified, I immediately wrote my letter of resignation, giving my supervisor immediate notification that my resignation became effective two weeks from today's date.

Since I would be resigning my employment with the local union on the island, I began to also plan my departure. I would be leaving the islands, returning to the mainland to conclude the education that I started seven years before. I was no longer interested in becoming a child psychologist, the passing of my mother helped me to come to his decision; it was as if I was studying this profession in an effort for her to show how much she loved me. Now that she was dead, my prospectus did a ninety-degree turnabout. I was no longer interested in my lifetime goal. What I would do or become was driven far away from my conscious mind. I knew that I wanted to continue with higher education because with a degree in any discipline would open doors to me, and without a degree, it would leave me powerless to demand my total worth in a culture that does or does not look to kindly on achievement by people of my ethnicity and cultural background.

Two weeks after I rendered my resignation from the Seafarer's International Union, my bags were packed and I was ready to begin another life adventure that I had left behind; after spending seven years at home. I returned to mainland New York where I had lived for fourteen years before my mother had departed from this life. I did not return to the Bronx, New York, but chose instead to spend time with friends who lived in Brooklyn, a borough that I had never lived nor visited. After spending a couple of days with friends, I was encouraged to come to Boston, Massachusetts, and with some hesitation and reluctance, I left Brooklyn, New York, and boarded a plane bound for Boston.

Chapter 14

My flight from New York J.F Kennedy Airport to Boston Logan Airport did not happen without incident, when I got off the airplane and stood at curbside, waiting for a taxi cab that would take me from Boston Logan to Esmond Street in Dorchester, Massachusetts. I got in to a cab (taxi) unintentionally leaving my movie camera bag with camera, personal belongings, and my wallet with my identification and all the money that I had. I did not lose all my monies since most of it had been deposited in a New York saving bank. My journey to Boston was further compounded by the idea that the individual who had invited me to come to Boston did not appraise anyone of my coming which caused some discomfort with myself, my ego, and me. I had never been at the mercy of anyone. Since I decided to leave my grandmother's home to travel abroad seeking to make a life on my own. After being placed in this awkward position. I was determined to hit the ground running in finding employment. Luck is not a thing I believed in, someone in a higher power must have been keeping a keen eye on me because the very next day, I went out seeking employment, and that very same day, I was able to secure employment with Sears Roebuck and Company. This employment was sort of transitioning me for better things, soon after becoming employed, another with better opportunities came my way and I grabbed it; my quest to get a better job and return to college was most paramount at this stage of my life.

I immediately enrolled in community college, spent one year there, and transferred my credits to the University of Massachusetts, Boston Campus. The University of Massachusetts was not a fit for my personality. Classes were too large, there were very little interactions with professors, and I believed that learning did not really take place with students enrolled at this university. Test administered by true and false and multiple choice did not measure learning, and after spending a year at the University of Massachusetts, I knew that I would not be able to continue to attend this University.

After summer break, I had investigated other colleges and Universities in the Boston Metropolitan area and found the college that would be conducive to my style of learning. Multiple choice exams, true and false quizzes did not measure learning, they were test and quizzes that measure short-term memory and in the fail in enrolled at Cambridge College in Cambridge, Massachusetts.

Learning at Cambridge College was measured differently from the previous colleges that I had attended. True and false and multiple choice question was replaced with case studies and problem studies. Students at Cambridge College were offered to opportunity to think critically and to develop psychological perspective in their everyday learning. This type of learning proved to be a refreshing change from the learning that we are so accustomed to beginning from the first grade through our senior year in high school.

My time at Cambridge College flew by a bit too fast; if I had enrolled a semester later, I would have been able to receive a master's degree in clinical psychology, but since I attended a semester earlier, I would have to settle for a master's degree in education/management. In order for me to have receive my degree, I was required to have maintained a 3.00 grade point average along with writing a master's project thesis, in all my three semesters at Cambridge College, I was determined to maintain a GPA of 3.00, during the last two semesters I began to work on my master thesis, who I titled "Understanding and Responding to the High Rate of Recidivism" among black youths a very important part of my curriculum at school because I worked as a Program Director for a youth services organization connected to the court system in Roxbury, Massachusetts. My thesis was develop through a questioner, for program officers in the juvenile justice system. And I interviewed a juvenile justice court judge. At the conclusion of completing the required thesis, it was submitted and approved by the select committee that approve and recommend students to attend their senior graduation and receive the accomplished Master's Degree.

My graduation on July of 1989 came, and once again, I was forced to attend without the benefit of my mother being there. It is unclear to me if she would have been there if she was still alive. It did not matter to me that my father was not there for my accomplishments; he was never a part of my growth and development, and even when I got to meet him in my early years, he had no interest in being a father to me. So once again, all that had developed with me, my struggles, my stumbles, and yes, my accomplishment were shared with friends who were very close to me.

Chapter 15

After spending many years living in Boston, Massachusetts, and after holding down responsible employment and after receiving my Master's Degree in Education and Management, I decided that it was time to once again spread my wings and fly. My eyes had been set on Atlanta, Georgia, for a very long time and after several visits and some vacation time. I relocated to Atlanta. Atlanta, Georgia, turned out to be one of the biggest mistakes that I had ever made in my life. Friends had always built Atlanta as a city for blacks with degrees. I was fooled by the hype; Atlanta might have been billed the city for blacks with degrees, but blacks with degrees did not include the black male.

Oftentimes, I've wondered about the movements in my life, the restlessness that I have always felt in the womb, to the cradle being delivered and the transition from my mother, to my maternal grandmother, then my paternal grandparents, but what I truly began to understand was that my life was destined to take me on a journey. And I am now on the journey that would never end. Individuals in the psychological profession might want to evaluate my behavior as troubling, but in accordance with biblical teaching, men's lives is predestined. We as human beings have limitations that have been determined by our creator. The theory of predestination is not a popular beliefs among non-religious individuals, but let's face it, could the highly developed world be a product or by product of evolution?

The Journey that Never End | 51

Atlanta, Georgia, like any other US city must be studied and evaluated before one can make a reasonably educated decision as move to that city or not to move. During my assessment and decision to relocate to Atlanta, I never really took the time to see Atlanta, Georgia, for what it truly was. The people seemed very nice, but being nice did not translate into how soon or how long employment could be gotten in a Southern City as compared to a city in all years of traveling from cities to cities, my most memorable memory of actually experiencing racial discrimination was in Atlanta, Georgia.

On one occasion, I was exploring the city on foot and subway, and I eventually found myself on the campus of Emory University Hospital Human Resources Department, and out of curiosity, I decided to glance through their employment wall where available and vacant jobs were posted. After identifying a position that I was well qualified to do, both education, and work experience, I approached a young white woman sitting in my presence, but simply replied to me that the Program Director's Position required that the applicant had/have a Bachelor's Degree, her attitude toward me left much to be desired, I therefore reiterated my interest in the position that I saw. Again she replied that the position required a bachelor's degree, which she assumed even before looking at me that I did not have the document required to be qualified for the position. After several minutes of attempting to engage this woman, who continued to ignore my presence, I finally asked her if a Master's Degree would allow me to apply for the Program Director's Position. She finally looked up and saw that I was a black man with an accent but not of Southern Origin. As if in shock and disappointment, she reluctantly gave me the employment packet, which I took and explained to her that the rest of my paperwork (resume, degree, and letters of recommendation) was at the hotel that I was staying on my visit to Atlanta, Georgia. Therefore, I had to leave and come back with all the pertinent information.

Within the hour, I returned to Emony University Hospital Campus to be confronted not by the white woman who gave me the employment application. This time, I was face to face with another bigoted individual. My second confrontation was now with an Asian American man, whose English was as broken as a scratch record, reiterated the same thing that his white counterpart had tried so desperately to tell me that the program director position requires a Bachelor's Degree, after minutes of exchanging pleasantries, I left Emory with the intent of not hearing from them ever again.

My struggles in Atlanta, Georgia, continued well into years that I did not have to spare and after my final bout with seeking gainful employment. I decided that my time in Atlanta had finally come to a screeching conclusion. This journey ended and another one willed itself into existence.

Chapter 16

After surviving three long years of non-productivity in Atlanta, my bags were packed and ready to head back to a city that was very good to me. Boston, Massachusetts, was a city that can be very cold in many more reasons than one; the people can be cold and standoffish, but it was a city that allowed me to dream, work, and be a productive member of its community. Just imagine living in a city, then moving away and then returning years later, to be given an opportunity to be given the job that was once vacated by you after three years had gone by and had to refused the position because funding sources and resources had be dramatically reduced. As I became re-acclimated to Boston, Massachusetts, my life moved on to greener pastures, I applied for a position with the Commonwealth of Massachusetts, the Department of Social Services and was hired as a social worker one, shortly after my employment. I was promoted to a social worker three step from a promotion to that of a program supervisor in the adolescent and children unit. Life was good, my brother (not blood related) and his two children were living in my home; his son, a very smart young boy, and a daughter who was premature at birth had some disabilities, she should have stayed with her mother who lived in the beautiful island of Antigua, the West Indies. As a social worker, I felt very uneasy with the idea of my brother being the primary caretaker of his daughter. As a parent, he was responsible for washing her skin, combing her hair, and dressing her appropriately to attend school. My brother and I had several arguments and discussions around his attempts to raise his daughter. We've gotten to the point where I have threatened to leave the household and go on my own, but to have left him alone with his children would have been suicidal, suicidal in the sense that he could hardly maintain a job. His skills were very limited, my leaving our home would have had detrimental effects on his children.

To further complicate the child-rearing process, the lifestyle that he was involved with was not conducive to his daughter who had emotional, psychological, and mental deficiencies. Yes! My brother was bisexual, he swings both ways, which was more reasons to send his daughter back to her mother, but after much discussion around this issue, he refused to listen to rhyme or reason. I could feel deep down in my gut that something terrible was going to happen and I told him on my fears, but he refused to listen to my concerns for his daughter's upbringing; he finally told me to bug off, he said and I quote, "he was not sending his daughter back home to live with her mother." The child's mother was not in a position to raise his daughter since she was already raising two older brothers. I should have ran as fast as I could from the situation that I found myself in, but I did not. The social worker in me saw the troubles that lay ahead for me so I waited for the ball to drop. Which brought to the idea that nothing that seems good last forever.

Several years went by, my brother's attitudes toward my concerns had not changed and got increasingly worst; my brother continued to refuse to send or even take his daughter back to the island of Antigua to live with her mother, feel on deaf ears.

Book Two

My life at this point in time have kept me wondering why I was chosen to be the recipient of such treatment that was handed down to me. I truly knew that there is a being who hears, sees, and knew everything; what was the purpose of me being in the body that I am in, was my life destined to where it ended? With the talents that was given me, how is it that I am not more than I am, with the voice that I possessed, along with my abilities in swimming, basketball, and the other sports that I had excelled in high school and even college, why had my life continued the way it had. Did my lack of parenting have any influence on my life or was there a reason why?

Chapter One

March 25 of any given year is generally the day that I celebrate my birthday, but on this particular day in 1994, I was not in the mood to celebrate now and have company over to my house. My workweek was coming to a screeching halt, but I needed to do my last best deed before my weekend began. On my agenda on this particular Friday was to do a supervised visit with two of my kids who were in foster care and their parents; my lunch break was scheduled from one p.m. until two p.m. and the supervised visit was from two p.m. until four p.m. On my lunch hour, I took the liberty of going to the package store to purchase a taste (liquor) that I might have to celebrate another year on planet earth.

At the conclusion of my supervised visit with the parents and their two children, I took both of the children back to their respective foster care programs (homes), and since this happened on a Friday afternoon, I did not go back to my office located in the field corner in Dorchester, Massachusetts. When I got home, I took a drink and headed to my bedroom where almost instantly, I fell into a deep slumber, only to be awakened hours later to voices coming from the kitchen area of my apartment.

The night of March 25 and the morning of March 26 is a day that would continue to ring a bell in my life, so much had happened that it would take another book to explain all that had happened, but to give my readers some perspective on that night and following morning would take almost forever, but nonetheless, my brother (play brother) was arrested by the Boston Police Department, he was charged with several counts of child abuse and molestation. His daughter, a minor, was removed from the home, but his minor son, they left. The Department of Social Welfare left in my home only to later file a SIA that claimed that I had sexually molested and abused my children. Thank God, I was hired as a social worker and had some experience with handling these kinds of problems as they arise. Why would the Department of Social Services leave a minor child in my home after arresting and prosecuting their father, removing the daughter, but leaving the son in my home, and ultimately filing a SIA against me for abusing and sexually molesting my children, the same children whom they accused their father of the same alleged crime that they were now accusing me of.

The harassment continued until the Department of Social Welfare along with their wacky attorney, and the attorney general's office decided to go before the court (juvenile court) in an effort to get the court to get a warrant for my arrest for sexually molesting and abusing a client's children. This attempt failed since the judge who they went before seeking this warrant was quiet familiar with my work as a social worker with the same department, who had convicted my brother (my friend) for the same crime mouths before.

My strong belief in God got me through the hoops that the state of Massachusetts was attempting to put me through, including the agency that I worked for. The apartment of Social Welfare, the then Governor of Massachusetts also had his say in the matter. He tried to use me as a political pawn, being an election year, he spoke to the media about my social work practice; he did not know me from a hole in the wall but became an instant authority on my character and work habits. He indicated that I was a poor excuse for a social worker and told whomever had the time to listen to his hog wash, that I had fallen through the cracks when, in essence, I was one of the best social worker that the department have hired in years. My social worker practice and work ethics could be seen by my numerous letters of perfect attendance along with my records of my contact with the families that was assigned to my case load. After I was terminated from position as a social worker III with the

Department of Social Services. My case records were transferred to other social workers at the field corner office in Dorchester, Massachusetts; workers were enthused by the manner by which my records were kept up-to-date.

Chapter Two

My brother (my friend) was convicted of a crime he did not commit; he was charged with a crime based on allegation made by a gay man whose demeanor presented the attitude of a drag queen more so than a gay man. His lies stemmed from the early morning affair that happened in my home the morning following my birthday of March 25. My brother and I was truly fluid with our sexuality, and if they had tried to prosecute him for the activity that took place in my home, it might have been harder to get a conviction for the actual stuff that took place. Nonetheless, my roommate, my brother, my friend, and even some said my lover was sent to jail and was soon after transferred to a Virginia prison. That took him far away from friends and family, and eventually after about ten years of incarceration, he died.

After his death, the, Virginia Department of Correction contacted me. Since I was listed on his prison documents, they shipped his dead body back to Boston, Massachusetts, to a funeral home that was specified by his brother (me). As small funeral service was conducted and as per directions, from his loving sister in Antigua, WI, his body was cremated, and the remains given to the son he had raised from the age of two.

His death in prison left some of his loved ones distraught, but the sister that was close to him and the one he helped to leave her husband in Saint Croix: (1) the US Virgin Islands and moved with him and his brother, his friend and his lover in Boston*, along with three children, (2)could have prevented her brother from going to sail, but refused to help, saying that she could not take time off from her job to go before the judge and take custody of her niece, her brother's daughter. Yet she claimed to be a Christian woman who attends church seven days a week but could not keep her youngest son out of sails.

After her brother's death in prison, his sister continued with her life as she did even before his death and after his incarceration.

Needless to say, my employment was terminated with the Department of Social Services. Friends who thought they knew me and claimed their love for me slowly disappeared from my life after the headlines exploded on the local newspapers of Boston, Massachusetts. I was not going to curl up nor was I going to soil over and die. I knew that the allegations of sexual abuse and sexual assault brought on by DSS and the attorney general's office was based on lies. I had no reason to be fearful since I had neither sexually molested my brother's children nor did I ever had any reasons to neglect them.

Chapter Three

After the big blow out in the local newspaper regarding the alleged crime that was committed, I began to gather my thoughts as to what I would begin to do with my life; jobs were not hard to come by, and since I was an articulate young person that also had a master's degree, finding a job was like easy as pie. After all, I was not convicted of any crime, and although the commonwealth of Massachusetts (i.e., the attorney general's office and the Department of Social Services tried to implicate me in the crime that they had convicted my brother, my friend and according to some, my lover, their attempts failed).

My friend's death have brought me to realizing that there are friends and friendships. That can last for a lifetime, and still there are so-called friends who are not friends at all, prior to meeting my deceased brother, I was pretty much a person who never really put much stock in friendships, but knowing him for that period of time, I sort of got away from my loathsome self. He was the life of everyone's party, some people hated him because he was very outspoken and oftentimes spoke what was on his mind. I loved him as my brother, my friend, and if I was looking for a lover, he would have been the ideal person to engage in a relationship with.

Overtime, my life did a complete ninety degree turnaround. It was always my desire to get in tune with religion but was hindered because of my involvement with my brother. I've often tried to encourage him to get back into his religion, and oftentimes, he would refuse; he would simply say, "I have been there." It was unclear what he was trying to say but realizing that he was a teacher and a preacher, I finally understood what he was saying. My brother, my friend, and possibly my lover (according to individuals in my life) had lost belief in God and my intentions to get him back on track with re-examining his beliefs and trust was beyond reach.

    His incarceration and eventual death in person turned my life inside out and upside down; it left me with a bitter taste in my mouth toward law enforcement agency since it was and still is my beliefs that law enforcement along with the governor of Massachusetts did not investigate the alleged crime that they accused my buddy of. It was a political year; the governor was under pressure by the citizens of the commonwealth and the department was under scrutiny for the manner by which children were being abused even in foster care. A friend I believe was made the fall guy, and each of these agencies rushed to judgment and convicted an innocent man for providing the best care that a single parent could provide for his children.

Chapter Four

I have always lived a quiet life, slow moving, minding my business and working my fingers to the bone in an effort to provide for my own existence here on planet earth. Never in the simple life that I've lived, have I ever imagine seeing my life dissected in the local tabloids: "Headline, Headline, read all about it, DSS Social Worker falls through the crack"; headlines detailed the allegations of sexual abuse on a minor child(ren). This incident allegedly happened the weekend of my birthday. This birthday happened so long ago, that memory does not really serve as to how old I was when this claim to fame and media exposure occurred, but a lie skyrocketed into the demise of a man who loved his children and his family and almost destroyed the life of his friend who was forced to endure the shame and humiliation of a story that was basically created by an individual who was left out of an orgy created by his friend my brother and an unnamed friend of mine. I excluded myself from the orgy even though it was my birthday. The participants to the orgy was simply my cup of tea, and as a result, I reframed from involving myself. This individual was left totally out of the loop and sought to penalize the host of the orgy, my brother for his indiscretion.

All alone in my bedroom, the liar came into my room, got into my bed and proceeded to play with my manhood; not really into his manipulation of my private part, I politely told him to stop and please leave my room, which further annoyed him; he gathered himself together, found his friend who had brought him to my home, and told his friend that he was ready to leave. His friend was apparently enjoying the orgy and refused to leave with him, and he began to exit the apartment, he murmured to his friend that "Someone was going to be sorry for what he was going to do." He left his friend, not understanding what he meant.

My brother and myself found out much later in the weekend what he meant; he went to the cops and told the cops that he had been to this house and that the occupant of this particular apartment had offered him money to have sex with his eight-year-old daughter. A lie that started the skyrocketing of my brother's involvement with the powers that be and the beginning of my inclusion into the horrid mess with my employment, my employers, and the systems in Boston, Massachusetts.

The culture here in North America is so different and at times unfair in the way they treat single parents versus married people, and it is so much more different in the way they treat single fathers raising their children as that of single mothers; here in America, there exists a double standard of people of color and sexual orientation Versus that of the population that coined themselves as straight. Although my life during this period in time was at a new low, my determination to stay on track with life and what the future may or may not hold was of paramount importance to me. I felt down but was not ready to count out.

Chapter Five

After surviving the shock at my so-called friends' rejection of me and the involvement that occurred allegedly at my home on that dreadful night of my birthday; it was now time for me to get back on the horse that had thrown me off. I quickly became involved with attending church and made all efforts to get back to my spiritual roots; next I began to seek employment opportunities that were conducive to my employment experiences and my degree requirement.

After months of pounding the employment circuit, I landed a counseling appointment with veterans' benefit clearing house. My responsibilities in this visible position was to provide services to veterans who were incarcerated and who were released from prisoners. Most of these released ex-offenders required employment/job training and a stable place to live. Some required help with obtaining veterans' benefits due to their services with the armed services of the United States, and still others required help in obtaining their honorable/dishonorable discharge with the veterans' ex-offenders was a rewarding experience for me. It also forced me to realize that my friend would never become an ex-offender. Since he was given a life sentence with no possibility of parole. And knowing this, my life took on other meanings. The once shaded person was now opened to whatever unexpected occurrence would have on my life. Religion became a more integral part of my daily life. The word *luck* began to diminish from my vocabulary, and faith, patience, and waiting became my mantra.

My trust in humankind was lost and replaced in my beliefs in a higher power. That higher power is God. I had not met him but was hoping that with my renewed involvement with my church, my pastor, and my brothers and sisters in the faith. I began to pray and seek the face of Lord and Savior. Because of all the incidents that surrounded my life, I thought it best to follow the teachings of the Bible in hopes of learning more of my destiny and the plans that God had for my life.

Chapter Six

After losing my one and only friend to prison and eventually death, I found a friend, his name is Jesus and he taught me that he will never leave me nor forsake me. I slowly began to put my life back on the journey that would never end. Work, church, work, church became the major focus of my life. I had no room in my life for the drama that most people would want for you to have in your lives.

Life went on for me, and although I was never one to crowd my life with all kinds of friends and acquaintances, I continued to live my life as a recluse. My experience with my last friend had encouraged me to be very wary of the people who wanted to surround themselves in a friendship with me. The teaching I inhabited from my mother who almost and always scrutinized the friends that I would bring to her house. As I reflect back on my mother and the way she treated my classmates when they came to visit me at her home, I oftentimes wondered how she was able to weed out friends from enemies. Most of my acquaintances would say that they were my friend, but my mother would correct them and most of the times, she would say to them that they were not friends.

My mother had lived a life void of love; her mother also had numerous children but no real man or lover in her life. Neither of these women seemed to be able to talk or discuss what it meant to be in love. My mother it seemed lost the ability to express her love for her son after the abandonment of her lover at six months pregnant.

The things that my mother did for me clearly told me that she loved me, but her inability to speak that love to me made me question a genuine love that a mother should have for her child or children.

What is love? And how important is it on having adults and even children to understand what basic emotion(s) are all about love as I would define it is an emotion that is innate; it is not like a subject that we can learn from but is something that each individual is born with and is slowly developed as one begins the aging process.

Chapter Seven

My adventures were great. I have moved and live in cities that I never dreamed that I would either lived or visit. I was never a dreamer, and I probably never realized nor understand what it meant to have a dream and set goals that you might want to set for yourselves. Goals, dreams, and aspirations came my way soon after I had completed my high school education. I knew that I wanted to get away from my island home and see how people outside my world live. When I initially began to attend City University of New York and after declaring a curriculum in Liberal Arts and Science, and after several courses in Psychology, it was determined that I would pursue a degree in child clinical psychology; this decision was made due to my birth, early development abandonment, and struggles with what life had given me.

As I slowly journeyed through this journey, my struggles continued working days in an effort to secure a degree by attending school at night and at times securing employment in the evening that I may attend college in the day in order to shorten the period between working and achieving a degree that could quite possibly change my whole life.

After attending city college for almost three years, I was finally able to secure permanent employment in the evening, thus affording me the opportunity to attend my Senior College at Herberth Lehman College located in the Bronx, New York. Classes at Lehman College started at eight a.m. and ran through two p.m. I had no college life, I ran from my classes at 2 p.m. to catch a train to get to work at 3 p.m. at times I often wondered if I would be able to accomplish the dream enrolling in college, so many children and young adults were more fortunate than I was, and even though I needed the moral support of my mother, I could not depend on her for finances, she could barely take care of her own needs, and thus I was privileged in attending college and working a job to provide for my financial needs. I guess I was a blessed child. However blessed I was, the road and journey that was before me was proving to be a long and hard road that I had elected to follow.

At my new institution of higher education (Herman Lehman College) where I began preparation to receive my Bachelor's Degree in the Science (Child Development Psychology). My studies were great, my grades were good, things seemed to be moving in the direction that I wanted them to be. My coworker and some of my supervisors were pleased with my abilities to attend college and especially in day school while holding down a full-time job in the evening, but sometimes, things seemed to be too good to be true and out of the clear blue. I woke up one morning to have my goals, dreams, and aspiration come tumbling down the hill, with twenty (20) credits away from my degree requirements my world came crashing down around me. On November 9, 1979, I woke up from my bed, bags packed to travel for the weekend to our nation's capital, Washington, DC. Having woke up to early to begin my weekend plans, I went back to bed and instantly fell into a deep sleep. While in this stage of sleep, I found myself surrounded by sharks. I found myself swimming on the bay where I was brought up in the US Virgin Islands. The shark surrounded me, and eventually, one of the sharks launched after me. By some stroke of my imagination, I avoided the shark's approach, and suddenly, the shark spoke. It said to me, "I did not get you this time, but I will and one of sharks bit me. The shark bit me on the right leg, and I woke up rubbing my leg where the shark had bitten me. This was a nightmare from hell, and it only got worse. As I began to get my bearings as to the episode surrounding my encounter with the sharks, my telephone rang.

The ringing of the telephone snapped me out of the nightmare that I was having so I answered it, only to hear a voice on the other end that I really did not want to hear. That voice was that of my aunt's husband, who I really didn't care for; right away, he began to tell me about being the bearer of bad news, over and over he ranted about being the bearer of bad news, and after being tired of his ranting, I told him if he did not tell me what the bad news was, that I was going to hang up my telephone, and with a deep sigh, he finally gave me the bad news. He told me instantly that I had just lost my mother. I thanked him as if he had offered me a compliment and hung up my phone. As I sat on my couch, it finally it hit me what my aunt's husband had just said to me. The voice in my head asked me if I had heard what this man had just told me. Then I finally understood that my mother had just passed (died).

With my planned trip ruined, I was now in the process of returning to my island home to bury my mother. To say that I was prepared for this undertaking would be an understatement, no one is ever prepared to face death at its ultimate, the process of separating myself from the love I always wanted but never got had begun to take shape; never in my wildest dream had I envisioned separating myself from the passing of my mother would take me seven years, but we never get over the loss of our loved one, and after still so many years, I still wonder if she truly loved me. She had always showed her love for me, but never in my whole life had she ever expressed verbally that love.

Chapter Eight

After many years (7) in the Virgin Islands (Saint Thomas) and working as a Union Business Agent with the United Industrial Worker of the Seafarer's International Union, I came head on with a work-related situation at my Company. I was faced with a contract violation that I oftentimes had to fight for the members that the Union Represented. Equal pay for equal work, in accordance with contract obligations, female members are paid and should be paid equally as their male counterparts if they are working in the same job and same classification.

One Union business representative (female) was hired to work and do the same job, but was paid exceedingly more money than I. This individual did not have the experience nor qualification that I possessed but was hired at a rate that was ten thousand dollars a year more that I was making. All attempts to resolve this major issue at the local level failed. My supervisor indicated to me that he was unable to do anything about it; his manager refused to discuss it and I was left to take the matter to the International Level.

After investigating the matter, it was learned that the young woman who was hired was also sleeping with the National Vice President. The National Vice President was getting two for the price of one. It was surprising to me even back then. That women would allow themselves to be used and abused by men who had no respect for themselves. My lost faith in the union and my abilities to not want me to function in the capacity that I would have to function forced me to say adios to a job that I truly loved.

Once back in the continental United States, I was encouraged to come to Boston, Massachusetts. I was told it was a state that was good if one was planning to pursue a degree in higher education. So off I went although. I heard about the racism in Boston, Massachusetts, I never allowed it to deter me from what I wanted out of life. Since my mother's passing and after spending time in my homeland. It was time to pursue my degree. All my plans to pursue a master's in child psychology and possibly a Doctorate in the discipline changed after the death of my mother. It seemed as If I wanted to become a doctor of psychology in an effort to get my mother to love me more and perhaps to hear her say how much she loved me, but knowing that I would never hear it from her because of her death, I immediately abandoned that dream, it was as if I was doing what I wanted to do for her and not for the betterment of self.

As my journey continued, I enrolled back into several colleges in Boston, Massachusetts, but being dissatisfied with their teaching methods, I became annoyed with how learning was measured. Learning to me was not taking true and false examinations, multiple choice questions was primarily based on the ability to recall things and circumstance through short- or long-term memory. After I transferred to Cambridge College in Cambridge, Massachusetts. I truly understood what true learning was. Cambridge College my alma mater thought that learning was having the ability to critically analyze documents and situations and come up with solutions after analyzing the same. Examinations was administered to students who were forced to analyze organization issues and other problem and define the measures needed to fix problems. Their learning modules was based entirely on the students' natural abilities to read, analyze, and to think critically on the everyday problems of life.

My attendance at this institution of higher education lasted for one year and six months graduating with a Master's Degree in Education with a major Concentration in Management.

Chapter Nine

After spending many years in Boston, Massachusetts, and working in the area of child growth and development, juvenile delinquency, job development, client advocacy, and as a more recent development as a Director for and outreach and tracking program, I decided that I've had enough of New England's harsh winter seasons and left to relocate to the warm climate of the south. My choice of relocation was of course Atlanta, Georgia. After spending vacations and weekend trips, I decided to pack up my bags, baggage, and all my needed stuff and headed to College Park, Georgia. Where I had already located and paid first and last month's rent and security, I was also able to have my telephone, light, and gas turned on long before I moved to my new home. My self-determination may have been the most destructive thing in my life when I decided to take a year off from wiles and woes of not seeking employment for a year. I wanted a year of from sweating and toiling for anyone, soon after my year off, the economic climate did a downturn, companies and government was not hiring and with a degree in hand. I found myself accepting employment opportunities in areas that I did not want to be employed.

My struggles in Atlanta, Georgia, lasted for three years before I realized that Atlanta, Georgia, was not the place that I wanted to be, my memory of blatant racism occurred to me in Atlanta, Georgia. During this period in my life, everyone was under the impression that blacks with degrees could easily make it in Atlanta, Georgia, but I learned to late that the hype was, is not true. The truth of the matter is, was that black women with a degree was better able to secure employment over her male counterpart with a degree. I believed that the antebellum attitude and slave mentality of white Southerners preferred to put a black woman in charge of her people instead of a black male. They believed that the black female would be better equipped to handle and control her own people.

The straw that finally broke the camel back came after I submitted my resume for an advertised position as an associate with the Center for Disease (CDC). Although the interview went well and was deemed qualified for the position, landing this position with the CDC was not in the cards for me, being qualified simply meant that my name would be placed on a waiting list with other qualified applicants and then I would have to wait until my name came up on that specified list before I could be hired with the State of Georgia (Atlanta) in the position that I was deemed to be qualified for.

Having this latest news, I was more determined now to get as far away from this state. As I could. It has three years of disappointment in my life, but life goes on. The life that I ran away from three years prior to was the same life I was planning to return to. The cold weather, the stuffy people, and a new insight to racism and what it means to be a black man looking at life in all its true form.

Christmas Eve this year found me arriving once again in Boston, Massachusetts, and although I wasn't moving into my own space, I was fortunate to have been given shelter by someone who I had once given shelter too. I had never lived with anyone in all my experiences since leaving my grandmother's home one year after my high school graduation. In this space, my life was very uncomfortable, but in haste, I was quickly able to secure my own living space my job experience. Once I returned to Boston, Massachusetts, ranged from that of a department of Social Services Social Worker to that of an outreach counselor, working with veteran offenders and ex-offenders with veterans' benefit clearing house.

Along the journey that never ends has brought me through a number of experiences having a first feeling of abandonment by a mother whose love for a man (my father) left me at a lost for understanding what a father's love might or could have been, it is so unfortunate that after all the many, many years have passed, women still finds themselves in a position of having several child or children for men who have chosen to absent from the women that they claim to love soon after these women become pregnant and are totally in extinction after the birth of their child(ren) and continues to be in the rear view of their children as they struggle with who they are and the absence of a father figure in their lives.

Chapter Ten

My early development was not a troubling one, I was constantly reminded of who my father was, is. My mother never spoke about him, but neighbors who knew him spoke of him as being a good person. Hearing all the stuff about him made me think even less of him. I eventually met him at the age of thirteen year, but at that time, I felt as if I was a grown man. We did not get along, and after my summer vacation in New York City, I was glad to rid my thoughts of even meeting him. Some years later, he died. I refused to attend his going-home service and his burial. When I notified my mother of his passing, her sadness of the news and the comments that she made told me that she still cared deeply for a man who had abandoned her so many, many years before. She and I had a lengthy discussion about him. I thought that he was a louse of a man, but she insisted that he was still in her sight a good man.

Many years had passed, when suddenly Luther Vandross recorded a song, "Dance with My Father"; this record brought me back to memories of my father. We had never really have a serious discussion on anything why he left my mother six months pregnant. Why he never looked back to see if she was alive or dead, and even though I had made several attempts to get to know this man, my efforts failed. I have danced with my mother throughout all of life. She loved to dance, so whenever we had to chance to dance with each other, we did.

My mother was oftentimes accused of being cougar; a cougar as we know it today is a woman who chased after young men almost twice their age. The last incident I can recalled of a man accusing my mother of infatuation of chasing a young man. My mother's boyfriend, she, and I was at a social gathering (a dance), the band was playing a Latin song, and my mother loved Latin music, and since her boyfriend could not dance, and since she wanted to dance so badly, she found me speaking with my friends, grabbed me by the hands and started dancing with me. At the same time, one of her boyfriend's friend turned to him and said to him that his woman was on the dance floor having a great time with this young man. My mother's boyfriend immediately followed his friend back to the dance floor, saw my mother and I dancing, and busted out laughing; he grabbed his friend and introduced me to him and explained that his woman and her son were dancing and enjoying themselves, and he then walked away. It must have been embarrassing for his friend because he did not understand that his friend's woman had a son, who really existed but few people knew this since his woman's son had been living away from his mother's stateside.

Chapter Eleven

Back in Boston, Massachusetts, after spending several years in my native land (Saint Thomas, USVI) and desperately trying to come to the realization that my mother was now dead and buried, my life must continue to evolve. My life started out as a sprint that slowly developed in to a marathon. All of my life, it seemed that I had governed my life the way I chose. And of course, I realized even now that I may have governed and made all the decisions pertaining to my everyday living, my path was being directed by a higher power more powerful than anyone can imagine. I was not a religious fanatic, but I fully later realized that the higher power that surrounded my life is God.

Boston, Massachusetts, was not the ideal place that I wanted to be, but it was the place where I had experienced the most hardships in my life; nevertheless, it was also the place where I had most thoroughly enjoyed my educational goals and objectives of course. I did not receive a Doctorate and PHD in Psychology, but it helped me to achieve the highest honor of my aspiration. A master's degree in Education/Management helped me to function as a Program Director and later on as an advocate for an organization that provided human services to ex-offender and incarcerated veterans. Life and the journey continued to engulf me with the power to stay on that road.

On numerous occasions, my journey appeared to be disappearing from the realities of life, but God had a different plan for my life and I thank him daily for being the master of my life. But situations and things often changed, and as things change, we as individuals must change. We live in an unpredictable world, and as much as we plan for things to happen, almost plans don't always work out the way we want before my mother's life was suddenly cut short. I had always contended that I would go to college, get my PhD in Psychology, and return to my island paradise, hang my shingles on my office space walls and provide services to children and young adults who have had a sporadic upbringing that I had. I was never an abused nor neglected child, but I had suffered with issues ranging from child abandonment, parental love shortcoming, and had to rely on primarily my abilities to manage surviving without the supervision and advisement of an adult parent.

Chapter Twelve

The need and want to become a child psychologist stemmed from wanting to help the most needy, servicing others it seemed was ingrained in the fiber of my whole being. Many people, some from a nucleus family, some from broken marriages and even those from single parents, struggle to understand what their calling is/was, but almost instinctively, I knew that I was sent to serve others. When I reflect on my past and from a very early age, the employment that I was employed tells a story of service to humankind. My brief stint as a junior engineer. That eventually evolved into a nursing assistant that afforded me the opportunity to attend college and maintain my own living quarters and eventually the death of my mother that interrupted my college education returned to me back into the place where life really started. The aspiration to become my own boss as a psychologist faded with the death and burial of a mother that I loved and cherished eventually I returned to mainland New York and continued my journey to Boston, Massachusetts.

One would think that Boston might have been the final stop on this journey that never ends, but it was not and after several years in this area and after many jobs providing services to the most needy, tragedy struck; the company that was working for decided to merge with another human services agency. Fortunately for me, I was retained by the company's merger, but could not with this new company; it was horrendous. Working conditions were bad, I was unfortunately forced to resign my position and forced into disability.

While in disability, my health got even worst. I was hospitalized and eventually placed in intensive care. As I struggled to get better, I was invited to move to Maine; not fully aware of Maine and its quaint little towns, I ended up living with an acquaintance that I knew in Boston, now transplanted in feral Maine (New Gloucester). Needless to say, this arrangement did not work to well for me. I was a city fella at heart, country living was never a part of my general makeup. After one month of this unhappy living arrangement, I decided that I needed to get away from this environment. I went to the city (Portland, Maine), found a nice comfortable apartment, and immediately grew wings and flew away from New Gloucester, Maine.

Leaving rural Maine (New Gloucester) and moving to the city (Portland) was the most exciting thing that I have done in a very long spell. This move enabled me to once again take control of my life. As individuals, we should never have to have other individuals controlling and running our lives; in New Gloucester, the freedom to do my own banking, shopping for food, and even attempting to attend church was left to the person that I lived with. I was at the mercy of this individual moods and how they felt on any given day. I was powerless to do for myself since I had given my car to a charitable organization, but that situation also passed. My journey continued even though I had to leave behind the things that was attempting to control my existence.

Before leaving rural Maine, bound for the city of lights, I was told by my friend that I should forget knowing them. The wheels had fallen off the cart. That cart was now stuck on its bottom, and I was determined to get as far away from a friend who had used me for his self-fulfillment.

Chapter 000 Zero

The journey that never ends has been and continues to be one of enlightenment, intrigue, trials, encouragement and also discouragement. I have evolved from being a person of dependency to one of independency. This journey reminds me of being on a roller-coaster ride, the many twist and turns, the many ups and downs that I have been through oftentimes I would sit in awe! As people and individuals talk of their lives and how depressing it could get at times, but could never understand what it felt like to be depressed.

Many tears had been shed into reflation as to what might have been if I had been guided by individuals with a sense of caring and loving. At times, I feel like a motherless child. My life had been a life without the sense of a mother's love. Have you ever experienced living a life with family where love was never discussed, expressed, or shown well? It is not a good feeling, my life from the beginning of time consisted of primarily doing for myself of course; unknowing to myself, I was being helped by a power beyond my own imagination and really never understood what or who that power was, but as time went by and after suffering loss after loss, my perspective changed and religion and religious doctrines began to be formed in my whole being. I may not have been loved by mankind nor understood what it was/is until I finally began to understand what the love of God meant.

The loss of my mother, grandmother, aunts, uncles, and some cousins gave me a better understanding of what it meant to live in a world where love was nonexistent entirely in my life. My father whom I hardly knew and did not get a chance to know was a man that I felt remorse for, but I was able to continue to do whatever it was that would help me to realize who I was and eventually could become.

Chapter 002

Oftentimes, people would make assumptions about who I was and what an only child should look like. Some thought that since I was an only child that I was a spoiled brat and got and demanded what I wanted when I wanted it. Truth be told, I was never spoiled by my mother. My mother was a woman who was educated to the ways of the world. I don't recall what grade in school she had completed, but she was wiser beyond her years. I could never demand anything from her; it seemed that after giving birth to me and after losing the love of her life to the world, she grow up faster than could have been expected. Like most mothers, she was the breadwinner in this family, and although her wages were very small, she always provided for all of my needs, but in providing for my needs, I was constantly reminded that her needs was just as important as mine. She always insisted that her checks were small, rent had to be paid, and if and when she needed something that I would have to wait until she can give it to me. It was not until I was enrolled in college taking courses in Psychology that I realized what the hierarchy of needs were. She taught me at a very early age what it meant to delay gratification; also back in the days, she taught me to better understand the differences between the id, ego, and superego personality. As I became older and began to fall in like (love) for some people, I began to understand the personalities of the various people that I became involved with.

My first true love was gentle, kind, loving, and a free spirit; she was a mediator on the personality, and that is why for years, I could not get her out of my system.

My first wife on the other hand, in accordance with Sigmund Freud, a behavior specialist, represented the id personality; everything revolved around her, she constantly wanted. It was always me, me, me, and oftentimes I, never us or they. When I decided to make her my wife and invited my mother to attend our wedding, my mother at first was very happy for me; she was under the impression that I was about to get married to my first love, the one she knew and thought that I would be marrying. When she found that I was not marrying her girl, she thought that I was making a big mistake. I got married anyway and soon learned that I did in fact marry the wrong woman. We had in essence live together for a number of years. Got married after those many years of cohabiting together, and six months after our marriage, I had to walk away from the relationship.

Chapter 003

As the years flew by, my life along life's journey continued on the paths of involvement with one woman after another while maintaining my undying love for a woman whom I had met many, many years before. I must have been in the eighth grade when this gem came into my life and could not get her out of my system. She was and is the energy that I've always wanted, but it was the source of energy that I could not truly harness. Friends had warned me several years before. That she was out of my league, but I had never been in anybody's league; nonetheless, I continued to chase after the wind.

I had no idea where my life was leading me. So I continued on the journey that never ends, hanging with men, women, the Godly and the ungodly, and all the people that society considered to be outcast, I felt myself as being one of the people that society considered to be from the other side of the track. The love of life, her brother, had also told me to my face that I was from the other side of the track. He made it known to me that I was not good enough for his sister; he also claimed that I had a bad reputation. He claimed that I used and abused women, we did not run in the same circle, he was an uppity nigger who thought that because his father and mother ran a mini grocery/liquor store, he felt as if was better than I.

My journey has taken me places where individuals would not dare to go, I have gone to the slum areas, I have visited white areas where blacks don't normally wants to, my work has also included visiting veteran offenders incarcerated in penal institutions, men and women drug addicts, and gay, lesbians, and brothers on the down low. I have no idea what it is to do drugs but can empathize with the individuals who might have gotten themselves caught up in the madness of drugs and drug addiction.

Growing up, I could have been anything that I wanted to be. A screaming sissy, a brother on the down low, or anything that anyone would attack my game too. I have always had questions on the way my grandmother raised and brought me up; she always insisted that I should learn to cook, wash my clothes, starch and iron them, she insisted that my rooms should always neat and clean and bed well made up. During my later teenage years, I began to wonder if my maternal grandmother was preparing me to be a good housekeeper for a no-good husband. But as I began to question her reasons for her wanting to know how to do these things, she would explain that every man should be able to do these things for himself. She further exemplified that if a man cannot do these things, then he would be at the mercy of a woman who could not cook, clean, and keep her man clean and feed.

When I reflect on my upbringings in the Virgin Island and I look on my present living situation here in Portland, Maine, and the racial issues throughout these United States with policemen killing black men, women, and children, it scares the hell out of me. Understand that I am a black man living in a community of white people, some good and some bad. In this community, I live in constant fear of being stopped while driving my car and while walking to and from church. The racial divide has been since the beginning of time, and after seventy years on this planet, the situation has still not gotten any better.

Growing up in the islands, I have experienced the abuse of police officers who used their shields, guns, and billy clubs as weapons to scare the people who were most vulnerable to their approach. On occasions, I would find myself in confrontation with officers who were being abusive to men who had had too much to drink (rum) become drunk and bullied and abused by certain police officer(s).

When confronting these officers, in defense of the helpless, I would be told that if I wanted some of the same treatment, I can also get it. And after some lengthy conversation, I would oftentimes say to the police officer. To take him gun belt off, drop his shield on the ground, and release his billy club from his side and I would kick his ass. Most of the officers would refuse my offer since they knew that I would actually kick their butts. Many years later, I had a second run-in with a peace officer in Boston, Massachusetts. I was always told to stay far away from Massachusetts; people claimed that it was and perhaps still is a racist town, but my incident did not include a white police office, but a black officer who stopped my car for reasons that he refused to discuss with me. Nonetheless, he stopped me illegally and the only reason I could think of was the fact that I was a black man, driving a halfway decent car peddling drugs. My confrontation with him escalated to the point where he felt the need to put his hand on his gun. Anticipating that I would make the wrong move to justify his killing of an innocent car owner. Racism does not always come in the farm of black and white, but it also shows its ugly face with blacks on blacks. I am not afraid of police officers, and although they too have human feelings and come from parents as I do, I have always kept a bad taste in my mouth for them.

So much if not all of my journey have been in reflection of what was, what might have been, and the reality of what is. The advantage and disadvantages of what life has brought. I am a firm believer that man's life (our lives) has been predestined. While other believers believed in the theory of evolution, I did not evolved from and ape or any other animal. I am the product of a man's sperm and a woman's egg coming together and a superior being (God) completing the cycle of sperm and egg getting together.

We were all created equally, however, we were not all given the same gifts at creation. One for instance of this is a man's penis size. All men were not gifted with having large penises. Men and women were not all granted/gifted with blond hair and blue eyes and men and women were all given height, weight, and complexion differences. Some individuals were gifted with the ability to become doctors, lawyers, nurses and other high-powered individuals, while others were given the enablement of becoming bakers, cooks and service personnel. On becoming or reaching the age of mental maturity, I was strongly moved to become a child psychologist, but after the death of my mother, the need to become that quickly disappeared.

Along life's journey, there has been so many lessons learned and I have always been told that one should never look back on one's past. I have always thought that one must and should look back because in looking back, one is more likely to not repeat the mistakes that I been made in the past. Regrets don't always come easily, but my one and only that I have ever had was that my mother did not have a brother or a sister for me. I believe that children should always have a sibling because it fosters understanding, love, rivalry, and even confusion among brothers and sisters. Although I had two younger brothers on my father's side, I've always found myself in conflict with the brother who followed me in the birth order; he was a brother from another mother, my father's wife. My last conflict with David came as a result of him asking why I had been named after his father, and since his mother was afraid or even ashamed to tell him what the facts of life was, I took the liberty to dump into their conversation, informing him that his father did not name me, but his grandmother did. She named me after her son because I was the spitting image of my father. Eventually, I invited David to the mirror and asked him to take a good look at himself, then look at his father, and then take a good look at me and see who most resembled the three pictures. Well, that observation finally shut his mouth up. David hated me on sight. I believe that after connecting with my father after thirteen years of my life, I believed that David thought in his mind that I had surfaced to cut his share of his father's good and well-being in half.

Eventually, his father died (our) and the relationship or lack thereof died. Thus, he and his brother Kenneth became a distant memory on this journey.

Chapter Five

My journey began in my native island of Saint Thomas, the US Virgin Islands; my primary education started out at the S. Antonio Jarvis Elementary School and I was held back in the first grade. My teacher, Mrs. Francis, told my mother that I was not ready to be promoted to the second grade; she indicated that I had not acquired the necessary skill in preschool nor kindergarten. Truth was I was never introduced to the areas of preschool nor kindergarten and therefore lack the skills in socialization, basic math, and reading and had to spend another school term in the first grade; on and on, my progress led me to the seventh grade where I landed at Charlotte Amalie High School. My high school years were exciting years. I met several young ladies and fell madly to love with the love of my life. Many mistakes occurred between us, and for many years, we were in and out of each other's life. Ultimately, I had to come to the realization that we could not be together. Her husband and her two children became a barrier to any possibility of us getting together to share the twilights of our remaining years together.

I have no idea of where this journey that never ends will eventually conclude, and after having traveled the world, Africa, the Dominican Republic, Europe, the Caribbean, Washington, DC, Virginia, New York, Boston, Massachusetts, and now Portland, Maine. I have enjoyed a life of hard work, pleasures, and leisure.

Every awakening moment in my life, I reflect back to the times that I have spent with my mother and in retrospect. I miss her more and more each day; life seems to become more difficult every day, but I thank my maker for carrying me along life's way.

Chapter Six

There have been so many meaningful things that have happened on my journey, and it surprises me to learn that our lives end almost the same way it begins. I was a child abandoned even before it was born, and the abandonment continued throughout my young life. I must have been almost five years old when my mother resurfaced back into my life and never finally meet my father until I was about the age of thirteen. So much of my young life had been shaped by a power that was beyond human comprehension and belief. The benefits of having my father and mother in my life during the most formative years of my life had been lost. Those were years that I could never get back so life and journey went on.

I don't mean to take my readers down memory lane with me, but so much of my life and other people's lives are parallel what I had gone through that I feel it imperative to share my experiences with my readers. Most of my readers have already learned that I was a child abandoned by my father and my mother; they have also understood that my maternal grandmother was left with the responsibilities of raising a child belonging to her daughter who disappeared from her young son's life because of her inability to parent her own offspring. Again, I was uprooted and abandoned by my maternal grandmother and sent away. There must have been someone guiding my life because even though I had been abandoned, I was never emotionally abused. I was not sexually abused by anyone during the years of my transitions, and I assigned that to a God that I did not know.

My upbringing in the US Virginia Islands was a simple one. I was never afforded the opportunity to attend a preschool, pre-K, nor a kindergarten school. When I got started in school, I started out in the first grade. When I finally matriculated to the sixth grade, there were no middle school ,and I matriculated to my high school that started from the seventh grade since there were no junior high school on the island.

My transition from the sixth grade to seventh grade threw me among students who were much older than I was; it brought me into contact with seniors and juniors alike. It brought me into contact with young women and women who were school age younger or older than myself. My very first school year, I tried out for every varsity school teams that they had at Charlotte Amalie High School; I played basketball, volleyball, football (flag), and I eventually joined the swim team. With a little guidance in these sports, I could have been a Lebron James in basketball; my fade-away jump shot from any area on the court was awesome. I could have been a Mark Spitz or even a Michael Phelps since I had a good understanding of all the swim strokes that are in use today.

Chapter Seven

I was never good enough according to the individuals who I was surrounded by. My enemies and friends despised the very ground that I walked on. My family members criticized my struggles and determination to do something better with my life and some often talk behind my back and wondered among themselves what was I trying to prove by successfully completing the JBM courses that I had taken and being enrolled at a Junior College. My determination to become the first member of my family to attend and graduate a University was of utmost importance to my life. My desires to attain a PhD in child psychology was lost soon after the death of my mother on November 9, 1979. After her death, it took me seven years to get my life back in order, and soon after returning stateside, I immediately enrolled back in college and received a Master's Degree in Education with a minor in management.

All of my working adult life, I was drawn to providing services to individuals who desperately needed advice, guidance, and even counseling while I myself needed to resolve my issues with abandonment. I've often wondered what it would have been like to have dreams and aspirations, but with the life I had as a child, there was never a reason to dream.

My last trip to my island home was in June of 2017; my return on this particular date (June 14 through June 24) was primarily due to my fiftieth high school class reunion. Fifty years away from young adults that I had attended high school with and so many faces that I could piece together but names I could not remember. Some friends could not understand when I commented on never having a desire to live on the island again. This feeling stemmed from my observation of the people who had never left the islands. Some friends and even acquaintances had become distant. The island culture had not changed; after fifty years away from the island of my birth, things had remained constant. At times, the islands was oftentimes pitched into sudden darkness, electrical current often cut off without warning and would be out for hours on end. Food is often so expensive that consumers would have to do without and salaries are so low, it discourages young adults to return back home to share their experiences with their own people. Politics on the island is almost as identical to that of the mainland. It is no longer what you know, it is who you know. Acquiring a degree from the main land and securing employment at home becomes a difficulty if you're not affiliated with the party in control in the Virgin Islands.

Chapter Eight

Soon after my departure from the island of Saint Thomas and at the conclusion of the activities of my High School Class reunion, the hurricane seasons began. Hurricane Irma began its descent on the Virgin Islands and opened the door to Maria, whose devastation left the island with a lack of clean water. Food and people been moved from a hospital that could no longer provide for the care that they so desperately needed, then you have a commonwealth country (Puerto Rico) who towns have suffered with devastation that no one would want to write home about and a callous president who sits back and does nothing for American citizens in need but constantly get involved with other people's business.

I am an American citizen. I am not a dreamer who was brought to USA by my parents, but I am a black man living in an America, but it is as scary being a black man in America as it is being a dreamer. This journey that never ends is real. I have no understanding of where this journey will lead me to. Portland, Maine, is not the wrap-up phase of the journey, and only God knows what or where the journey would take me.

Descriptions of the characters:

Iva Vanterpool (maternal grandmother) was a woman of four feet five inches tall; she was light complexioned, shapely with steel-blue cat eyes. A woman who kept exclusively to herself. It is ironic that this woman gave birth to nine children without the benefit of marriage to none of her nine children's fathers.

My eldest Aunt Glady George-Thourbourne was married and had no children' she lived all of or most of her life living in the city of New York where she attended cosmetology school, became a beautician, and did odd jobs working in New York's finest hospitality establishments.

Benito Hernandez, my eldest uncle, joined the military (army) in the late fifties; when he enlisted, he changed his name from Benito Amos to Benito Hernandez. Benito joined the fire department of the Virgin Islands.

Rehalio Smith, a less fortunate uncle, was born a product of his own making, refusing to attend primary school; he never learned to read nor write and was left at the mercy of a woman who eventually became his wife and who eventually began to end his life.

Next on the food chain was my mother, Anita Amos. My mother Anita was a woman of stature, somewhat tall, five feet eight inches. Dark complexioned and shapely like her mother. From the onset, it appeared this rather nice no-nonsense woman would have no luck with men, beginning with the treatment of my father (as told in the novel) and ending with death of one her lovers and eventually of her own demise.

Then there was Alexander Smith, better known to his older brother and sisters as Kay Kay. Not much is known of him, except that he took ill, was taken to the local hospital in Saint Thomas the US Virgin Islands where he was given an injection, and shortly thereafter died with no reasonable explanation as to why.

Corina Chinnery-Warner, Patricia Chinnery, and Irene Chinnery were all sisters born to my grandmother, Iva Vanterpool, and Reuben (Ben) Chinnery. No one truly understood the Chinnery sisters; it appeared at times that they hated the older siblings and were constantly at each other throats. They all had sons and daughters except the one named Irene Chinnery; eventually, they all died, leaving the loved ones to mourn their loss.

Next in line to come into this mix-up was my youngest aunt: Alicia Richards-Abrahamson, and like all the rest of her mother's daughters was just as shapely as the rest of her sisters. On my paternal grandparents side was my paternal grandmother: Mrs. Elizabeth Fraser (better known as Lizzie the Horse); she was called Lizzie the Hass because she resembled a thoroughbred. Then there is her husband Zacabrial Fraser, my grandfather who did not to help me when I was being dragged to and from the local burial ground.

Elizabeth and her husband had also became parents to Gustave, Luther, and a sister, Kethurah Fraser, Gustave, and his Luther (my father) left home at a very early age to get away from the problems that plagued them when they were children.

I would hopefully create more based on the title of this novel, *The Journey That Never Ends*. The attached named characters would play their famed characters; the individuals named are all deceased.

Property of Luther D. Fraser
13 Emerson St. #105
Portland, Maine 04101
207-518-9584

www.ingramcontent.com/pod-product-compliance
Lightning Source LLC
LaVergne TN
LVHW040108080526
838202LV00045B/3822